*R*each high, for stars lie hidden in
your soul. Dream deep, for every
dream precedes the goal.

— Pamela Vaull Starr

We wish to thank Susan Polis Schutz for permission to reprint the following writing that appears in this publication: "Give yourself freedom...." Copyright © 1989 by Stephen Schutz and Susan Polis Schutz. All rights reserved.

ISBN: 0-88396-847-9

ACKNOWLEDGMENTS appear on pages 4 and 48.

Certain trademarks are used under license.
BLUE MOUNTAIN PRESS is registered in U.S. Patent and Trademark Office.

Printed in the United States of America.
First Printing: 2004

 This book is printed on recycled paper.

This book is printed on fine quality, laid embossed, 80 lb. paper. This paper has been specially produced to be acid free (neutral pH) and contains no groundwood or unbleached pulp. It conforms with all the requirements of the American National Standards Institute, Inc., so as to ensure that this book will last and be enjoyed by future generations.

Blue Mountain Arts, Inc.

P.O. Box 4549, Boulder, Colorado 80306

WORDS THAT SHINE LIKE STARS

How to have the life you've always wanted... Advice from celebrities and wonderful others

Edited by Douglas Pagels

Blue Mountain Press™

Boulder, Colorado

ACKNOWLEDGMENTS

We gratefully acknowledge the permission granted by the following authors, publishers, and authors' representatives to reprint poems or excerpts from their publications.

Harcourt, Inc., for "Sailors used to..." from STARS TO STEER BY, edited by Louis Untermeyer. Copyright 1941 by Harcourt, Inc., and renewed 1969 by Louis Untermeyer. All rights reserved. And for "The little prince..." and "There was, on one..." from THE LITTLE PRINCE by Antoine de Saint-Exupéry. Copyright 1943 by Harcourt, Inc. Copyright renewed 1971 by Consuelo de Saint-Exupéry. English translation copyright © 2000 by Richard Howard. All rights reserved. And for "And fixing on..." from BRING ME A UNICORN: DIARIES AND LETTERS OF ANNE MORROW LINDBERGH 1922-1928 by Anne Morrow Lindbergh. Copyright © 1972 by Anne Morrow Lindbergh. All rights reserved. Dutton, a division of Penguin Putnam, Inc., for "'When you wake...'" and "'How would it be...'" from THE WORLD OF POOH by A. A. Milne. Copyright © 1957 by E. P. Dutton & Co., Inc. All rights reserved. And for "What matters..." from SO FAR... by Kelsey Grammer. Copyright © 1995 by Kelsey Grammer. All rights reserved. Mitchell Lane Publishers, Inc., for "The whole point..." by Keri Russell from KERI RUSSELL by Judy Hasday. Copyright © 2001 by Mitchell Lane Publishers. All rights reserved. Scrivener and Company, Publishers, for "People with ambition..." and "We might well..." from PATTERNS FOR SUCCESSFUL LIVING by Dan Custer. Copyright 1946 by Dan Custer. All rights reserved. Dorothy Parker for "The cure for boredom...." Copyright © by Dorothy Parker. All rights reserved. Henry Holt and Company for "For a moment..." from THE OUTERMOST HOUSE by Henry Beston. Copyright © 1928, 1949 by Henry Beston. Copyright renewed Henry Beston, 1956. Copyright renewed Elizabeth C. Beston, 1977. All rights reserved. Simon & Schuster Adult Publishing Group for "What I've learned..." from IT'S ALWAYS SOMETHING by Gilda Radner. Copyright © 1989 by Gilda Radner, copyright © renewed 1990 by The Estate of Gilda Radner. And for "The best advice..." from LETTERS TO JUDY by Judy Blume. Copyright © 1986 by Kids Fund. All rights reserved. Ballantine Books, a division of Random House, Inc., for "Share everything..." from ALL I REALLY NEED TO KNOW I LEARNED IN KINDERGARTEN by Robert Fulghum. Copyright © 1986, 1988 by Robert L. Fulghum. All rights reserved. And for "My philosophy is..." by Naomi Judd from LOVE CAN BUILD A BRIDGE by Naomi Judd. Copyright © 1993 by Naomi Judd. All rights reserved. And for "I think..." and "When I look..." from STILL ME by Christopher Reeve. Copyright © 1998 by Cambria Productions, Inc. All rights reserved. And for "We cannot always..." from DAYS OF GRACE by Arthur Ashe and Arnold Rampersad. Copyright © 1993 by Jeanne Moutoussany-Ashe and Arnold Rampersad. All rights reserved. Time & Life Publications for "What's very important..." by J. K. Rowling from "Hocus Focus: Millions of readers are falling under the spell of *Harry Potter and the Goblet of Fire*" (*Entertainment Weekly*: August 11, 2000, p.28). Copyright © 2000 by Time & Life Publications. All rights reserved. HarperCollins Publishers, Inc., for "There is a voice..." and "Woulda-Coulda-Shoulda" from FALLING UP by Shel Silverstein. Copyright © 1996 by Shel Silverstein. All rights reserved. And for "Tell yourself..." from YOUR ERRONEOUS ZONES by Dr. Wayne W. Dyer. Copyright © 1976 by Wayne W. Dyer. All rights reserved. And for "It would be nice..." from HOW TO LIVE BETWEEN OFFICE VISITS by Bernie S. Siegel, M.D. Copyright © 1993 by Bernie S. Siegel. All rights reserved. And for "Sometimes I lie..." from THE WORLD IS FILLED WITH MONDAYS by Charles M. Schultz. Copyright © 1999 by United Feature Syndicate, Inc. All rights reserved. And for "For fast-acting..." from THE SEARCH FOR INTELLIGENT LIFE IN THE UNIVERSE by Jane Wagner. Copyright © 1986 by Jane Wagner, Inc. All rights reserved. And for "My recipe for..." by Derek Jameson and "Being armed with..." by David Gee from THE RELAXATION LETTERS, compiled by Audrey Burns Ross. Copyright © 1993 by Audrey Burns Ross. All rights reserved. William Morrow and Company, Inc., a division of HarperCollins Publishers, for "We all have..." from THE ONE MINUTE SALES PERSON by Spencer Johnson, M.D. and Larry Wilson. Copyright © 1984 by Candle Communications Corporation. All rights reserved. And for "I can do..." and "If you come..." from WHOOPI GOLDBERG BOOK by Whoopi Goldberg. Copyright © 1997 by Whoopi Goldberg. All rights reserved. Thomas Nelson, Inc., Nashville, TN, for "Here's what I would..." from ZIGLAR ON SELLING by Zig Ziglar. Copyright © 1991 by Zig Ziglar. All rights reserved. Doubleday, a division of Random House, Inc., for "Remember always..." from YOU LEARN BY LIVING by Eleanor Roosevelt. Copyright © 1960 by Eleanor Roosevelt. All rights reserved. And for "Never lose..." by Gordon Dean from THEY ROSE ABOVE IT by Bob Considine. Copyright © 1977 by Millie Considine as Executive of the Estate of Bob Considine. All rights reserved. And for "Give of yourself..." by Anne Frank from DIARY OF A YOUNG GIRL, edited by Otto Frank and Mirjam Pressler, translated by Susan Massotty. Copyright © 1995 by Doubleday, a division of Random House, Inc. All rights reserved. Wm. B. Eerdmans Publishing Company for "A long and contemplative..." and "Reflecting for a few..." from PATHWAYS TO UNDERSTANDING by Harold E. Kohn. Copyright 1958 by Harold E. Kohn. All rights reserved. Random House, Inc., for "You have brains...," " Be sure when...," and "UNLESS someone..."

(Acknowledgments continued on page 48)

Contents

(Authors listed in order of first appearance)

Sailors used to set their course by a star.... The star showed them where they were, and brought them to their destination.

Good poems are like the Polestar. They are not merely flashes of light and color. They are more than flaming comets that cut through the heavens and light up the mind for a moment. They are fixed and steadfast; they inspire us; their light will not fail.... They are stars to steer by.

Don't expect me to tell you which are the passing meteors and which are the true fixed stars. You are the navigator; you must find them yourself.

Open the book and see.

— Louis Untermeyer

The little prince sat down on a rock and looked up into the sky. "I wonder," he said, "if the stars are lit up so that each of us can find his own, someday."

— Antoine de Saint-Exupéry

24 Things to Always Remember... and One Thing to Never Forget

Your presence is a present to the world ■ You're unique and one of a kind ■ Your life can be what you want it to be ■ Take the days just one at a time ■ Count your blessings, not your troubles ■ You'll make it through whatever comes along ■ Within you are so many answers ■ Understand, have courage, be strong ■ Don't put limits on yourself ■ So many dreams are waiting to be realized ■ Decisions are too important to leave to chance ■ Reach for your peak, your goal, your prize ■ Nothing wastes more energy than worrying ■ The longer one carries a problem, the heavier it gets ■ Don't take things too seriously ■ Live a life of serenity, not a life of regrets ■ Remember that a little love goes a long way ■ Remember that a lot goes forever ■ Remember that friendship is a wise investment ■ Life's treasures are people... together ■ Realize that it's never too late ■ Do ordinary things in an extraordinary way ■ Have health and hope and happiness ■ Take the time to wish upon a star ■

And don't ever forget...
    for even a day... how very special you are.

— Douglas Pagels

Be humble, for you are made of earth.
Be noble, for you are made of stars.

— Old Proverb

There is something sublime about the beginning of a new day.... The fresh beginning of a new day, with its beautiful light and its promise of unexplored possibilities, should gladden the heart and inspire the soul.

— Grenville Kleiser

"When you wake up in the morning, Pooh," said Piglet at last, "what's the first thing you say to yourself?"

"What's for breakfast?" said Pooh. "What do *you* say, Piglet?"

"I say, I wonder what's going to happen exciting *today*?" said Piglet.

Pooh nodded thoughtfully.

— A. A. Milne

The whole point of life is to experience a little bit of everything, and I think it's better when there are a few surprises thrown in.

— Keri Russell

Watch the worlds come twinkling into view, first one by one, and the myriads that no man can count, and lo! the universe is white with them; and you and I are here.

— Marco Morrow

People with ambition live more years and each one of their years means more for they live more fully. When people say they get tired of life, it means, of course, that they are tired of the place they occupy, tired of doing the same thing, tired of seeing and being the same person. Such people are in a rut. Generally when we get tired it is because we are bored.

— Dan Custer

The cure for boredom is curiosity.
There is no cure for curiosity.

— Dorothy Parker

I have never been bored an hour in my life. I get up every morning wondering what new strange glamorous thing is going to happen and it happens at fairly regular intervals. Lady Luck has been good to me and I fancy she has been good to every one. Only some people are dour, and when she gives them the come hither with her eyes, they look down or turn away and lift an eyebrow. But me, I give her the wink and away we go.

— William Allen White

For a moment of night we have a glimpse of ourselves and of our world islanded in its stream of stars.

— Henry Beston

What I've learned the hard way is that there's always something you can do. It may not be an easy thing to do.... But there is always something you can do.

— Gilda Radner

What's very important for me is when Dumbledore says that you have to choose between what is right and what is easy.... All of them are going to have to choose, because what is easy is often not right.

— J. K. Rowling

There is a voice inside of you
That whispers all day long,
"I feel that this is right for me,
I know that *this* is wrong."
No teacher, preacher, parent, friend
Or wise man can decide
What's right for you — just listen to
The voice that speaks inside.

— Shel Silverstein

We all have all of the answers within us, if we just listen to ourselves.

— Spencer Johnson, M.D.

Even a small star shines in the darkness.

— Finnish Proverb

Be yourself; an original is always better than a copy.

— Anonymous

Here's what I would love to say: "You are rare; you're special, unique, and important. You can make a difference in the lives of other people. Over ten billion people have walked the earth, but there is not now, there never has been, and there never will be another one quite like you. Your voice pattern is different from any other voice on earth; your fingerprints are different; your very genes leave their trail of identifying marks completely different from any human being who has ever lived. You're a special individual. Develop your uniqueness; apply it by using the principles we have been discussing and make a real effort to be a difference maker in other lives."

— Zig Ziglar

Remember always that you have not only the right to be an individual, you have an obligation to be one.

— Eleanor Roosevelt

A long and contemplative look at the stars suggests to a thoughtful person the need of shining in his own place, at his own magnitude, and with his own hue.

— Harold E. Kohn

Tell yourself it's O.K. if you don't know where you are going
at every moment of your life.... You don't have to know where
you're going — as long as you're on your way.

— Dr. Wayne W. Dyer

You have brains in your head.
You have feet in your shoes.
You can steer yourself
any direction you choose.

— Dr. Seuss

Give yourself freedom to try out new things
Don't be so set in your ways that you can't grow.

— Susan Polis Schutz

All things journey: sun and moon, morning, noon, and
afternoon, night and all her stars... We go with them!

— George Eliot

If you can walk, you can dance.
If you can talk, you can sing.

— Zimbabwean Proverb

You don't have to know *how* to sing. It's feeling as though you *want* to that makes the day worthwhile.

— Coleman Cox

I am not a person of moods. I am a person of *one* mood: good. I can be impatient and short-tempered when matters concerning me are handled badly, but these outbursts always have a specific cause (whether I am right or wrong). When the problem is resolved, I return quickly to my normal state: happy, optimistic, and at peace with the world.

— Luciano Pavarotti

Look up at the stars. Lift your voice and raise your spirits. And let your soul aspire higher.

— Douglas Pagels

There are times when life isn't all you want, but it's all you have. So what I say is: Have it! Stick a geranium in your hat and be happy!

— Anonymous

I set the timer for 6½ minutes to be lonely, and 22 minutes to feel sorry for myself. And then when the bell rings, I take a shower or a walk or a swim, or I cook something — and think about someone else.

— Joan Blondell

Speaking of recipes with courage and cheerfulness as ingredients, here's one that a friend sent in to me: "Keep your head cool, your feet warm, your mind busy. Don't worry over trifles. Plan your work ahead, then stick to it, rain or shine. Don't waste sympathy on yourself — if you are a gem, someone will find you. Don't whine. Tell people you are a failure and they will believe you. Talk and act like a winner and in time you will become one."

— Anonymous

How much beauty we would have missed if we had not remembered to look up.

— Ruth C. Ikerman

My recipe for success: to be absolutely sure what it is you want to do, to master your subject to the very best of your ability and then go for it with total dedication and enthusiasm. It helps to be lucky.

Brush aside stress and worry. If you slip down the ladder, grit your teeth and start climbing up all over again.

— Derek Jameson

Climb from where you are. Take the step that is next above you and wait for the one beyond to be revealed in its time. The ladder reaches somewhere; it must needs rest on something at the top. Believe and climb.

— George Landor Perin

Our thoughts are ladders by which we climb toward the things which hang above us — our ideals, whatever they are.

— Hermann Hagedorn

So be sure when you step.
Step with care and great tact
and remember that Life's
a Great Balancing Act.
And will you succeed?
Yes! You will, indeed!
(98 and ¾ percent guaranteed.)

— Dr. Seuss

Ideals are like stars... choose them as your guides, and following them you will reach your destiny.

— Carl Schurz

I think the ones who survive in life do it by hammering at it one day at a time. You do what you have to do to get through today, and that puts you in the best place tomorrow.

— Oprah Winfrey

Being armed with the twin philosophies of *Carpe Diem* ("Seize the day") and "Each day is the first day of the rest of your life" means that I am always trying to pack as much into each day as possible.

— David Gee

Don't waste time. If all of your life is ahead of you, plan to use it all, *and begin with the present hour....* Time slips through your fingers like sand through the fingers of a child on the seashore. Each grain of sand is an hour, and each handful is a year. What others have done you can do if you will. Time enough is still ahead of you. The last days are as good as the first if you refuse to believe in any difference. Whether your sun be rising or setting, use the hours of light and opportunity that remain.

— Arthur Brisbane

Life's a pretty precious and wonderful thing. You can't sit down and let it lap around you... you have to plunge into it; you have to dive through it! And you can't save it, you can't store it up; you can't hoard it in a vault. You've got to taste it; you've got to use it. The more you use the more you have... that's the miracle of it!

— Kyle Samuel Crichton

He who is bound to a star does not turn back.

— Leonardo da Vinci

People go abroad to wonder at the height of mountains, at the huge waves of the sea, at the long courses of the rivers, at the vast compasses of the ocean... and they pass by themselves without even imagining.

— Augustine of Hippo

We go through life as some tourists go through Europe — so anxious to see the next sight, the next cathedral, the next picture, the next mountain peak, that we never stop to fill our sense with the beauty of the present one.

— Minot J. Savage

"How would it be," said Pooh slowly, "if, as soon as we're out of sight of this Pit, we try to find it again?"

"What's the good of that?" said Rabbit.

"Well," said Pooh, "we keep looking for Home and not finding it, so I thought that if we looked for this Pit, we'd be sure not to find it, which would be a Good Thing, because then we might find something that we *weren't* looking for, which might be just what we *were* looking for, really."

— A. A. Milne

The light of a single star tinges the mountains of many regions.

— Chinese Maxim

It would be nice if we were each born with a manual on how to live, or were taught how to do so early in life by experts.

— Bernie Siegel, M.D.

Here's my Credo:

All I really need to know about how to live and what to do and how to be I learned in kindergarten.... These are the things I learned:

Share everything ■ Play fair ■ Don't hit people ■ Put things back where you found them ■ Clean up your own mess ■ Don't take things that aren't yours ■ Say you're sorry when you hurt somebody ■ Wash your hands before you eat ■ Flush ■ Warm cookies and cold milk are good for you ■ Live a balanced life — learn some and think some and draw and paint and sing and dance and play and work every day some ■ Take a nap every afternoon ■ When you go out into the world, watch out for traffic, hold hands, and stick together ■ Be aware of wonder ■ Remember the little seed in the Styrofoam cup: The roots go down and the plant goes up and nobody really knows how or why, but we are all like that ■ Goldfish and hamsters and white mice and even the little seed in the Styrofoam cup — they all die ■ So do we ■ And then remember the Dick-and-Jane books and the first word you learned — the biggest word of all — LOOK ■ Everything you need to know is in there somewhere ■

— Robert Fulghum

Blessings on your young courage, boy; that's the way to the stars.

— Virgil

It's never too late to have a happy childhood.

— Anonymous

There's nothing in the whole universe so intensely and immensely worth while as being you, with... the sky the limit.

— Gene Stratton Porter

My mantra has become, "Know no boundaries." This does not suggest reckless abandon, but an open mind that asks, "What would I attempt to do if I were sure I wouldn't fail?"

— Joan Lunden

The mind is like a parachute. It works best when it is open.

— Anonymous

And when the sun sets in the west...
a twinkling star pins itself upon a cloud.

— F. J. Worrall

We might well write out an affirmation and hang it over the desk or over the kitchen sink: I AM ALWAYS OPEN TO NEW IDEAS.

— Dan Custer

Here are some affirmations that have helped me. Use them if you'd like. They're yours free (except for what you paid for the book; if you borrowed this book from a friend or the library and you feel you should send me a few bucks, that's fine, too).

I'm a little teapot, short and stout. Here is my handle, here is my spout ■ I bet nobody knows I'm crazy ■ I look good in bell bottoms... ■ I can walk through walls. Ouch! No, I can't ■ I mean for my hair to look like this... ■ I don't need to exercise. I have the perfect shape ■ I'm smarter than my dogs. Well, smarter than one of my dogs... ■ It's not important to know what everybody else seems to know. I don't care how much they laugh at me... ■ If I put my mind to it, I could do anything. I just don't feel like putting my mind to something. So there... ■ I'm good at watching TV ■ I can come up with better affirmations than these ■

— Ellen DeGeneres

Take time every day to do something silly.

— Philipa Walker

Be glad of life because it gives you the chance to love and to work and to play and to look up at the stars.

— Henry van Dyke

We occasionally have times when the television and radio are off and all is quiet, we find ourselves alone with our thoughts. This golden opportunity affords us the privilege of a bit of self-evaluation. Are we living up to the highest and best within us? Are we getting the most out of life by giving our best? Are we entertaining only those thoughts which make good blueprints for living?

— Edward A. Beiersdorf

What more can be said today, regarding all the dark and tangled problems we face than: Let there be light.

— John F. Kennedy

Reflecting for a few moments upon what I consider to be life's basic essentials, I find the following are among the most fundamental (although I do not list them in order of their importance):

To live in such a way as to have nothing I wish to hide from God or man ■ To be tough with myself and tender with others ■ To face unpleasant facts unflinchingly ■ To love mankind all-inclusively ■ To be tolerant of others' religious and philosophical positions, knowing we may share the same experiences without having the same explanations of them ■ To live above minimums, doing more for the world than is demanded of me ■

— Harold E. Kohn

The darkest night the world has ever seen, did not put out the stars!

— Anonymous

Life is hard.
Next to what?

— Anonymous

Life is not easy for any of us. What does that matter? We must persevere and have confidence in ourselves. We must believe that our gifts were given to us for some purpose, and we must attain to that purpose, whatever the price we have to pay for it.

— Marie Curie

Each day comes bearing its gifts.
Untie the ribbons.

— Ann Schabacker

You can have *any*thing you want
but you can't have
*every*thing you want.

— John-Roger and
Peter McWilliams

You never enjoy the world aright... till you are clothed with the heavens and crowned with the stars.

— Thomas Traherne

I wish you some new love of lovely things, and some new forgetfulness of the teasing things, and some higher pride in the praising things, and some sweeter peace from the hurrying things, and some closer fence from the worrying things.

— John Ruskin

There's no greater luxury than doing what you want when you want to do it. I've lived the life I've wanted to.... I don't get down, even when I'm sick.... Now pass the peanuts.

— Katharine Hepburn

Sometimes I lie awake at night, and I think about the good life that I have... I really have no complaints...

Then a voice comes to me from out of the dark, "We appreciate your attitude!"

— Charlie Brown

And fixing on a star I grew...
— Anne Morrow Lindbergh

Sometimes it's important to work for that pot of gold. But other times it's essential to take time off and to make sure that your most important decision in the day simply consists of choosing which color to slide down on the rainbow.

— Douglas Pagels

For fast-acting relief try slowing down.

— Jane Wagner

Don't hurry, don't worry. You're only here for a short visit. So be sure to stop and smell the flowers.

— Walter Hagen

There is more to life than increasing its speed.

— Mahatma Gandhi

Teach me your mood, O patient stars!
Who climb each night the ancient sky.

— Park Benjamin

There are parts of a ship which taken by themselves would sink. The engine would sink. The propeller would sink. But when the parts of a ship are built together, they float. So with the events of my life. Some have been tragic. Some have been happy. But when they are built together, they form a craft that floats and is going someplace. And I am comforted.

— Ralph Sockman

Rivers hardly ever run in a straight line.
Rivers are willing to take ten thousand meanders
And enjoy every one and grow from every one —
When they leave a meander they are always more
Than when they entered it.
When rivers meet an obstacle,
They do not try to run over it;
They merely go around —
But they always get to the other side.
Rivers accept things as they are,
Conform to the shape they find the world in —
Yet nothing changes things more than rivers;
Rivers move even mountains into the sea.
Rivers hardly ever are in a hurry —
Yet is there anything more likely
To reach the point it sets out for than a river?

— James Dillet Freeman

Drop a pebble in the water and its ripples reach out far,
And the sunbeams dancing on them may reflect them to a star.

—Joseph Norris

Unshakeable confidence, a realistic goal, self-discipline, undaunted courage, love for one's fellowmen, and a reliance on an unfailing faith are a few of the buoys by day and the stars by night which guide us safely to a peaceful harbor.

— Edward A. Beiersdorf

Of all the lights you carry in your face,
Joy will reach the farthest out to sea.

— Henry Ward Beecher

What can be so far-reaching as a few quiet moments each day in which to turn inward in thought and to feel that one is part of a great whole? From within one finds reservoirs of inspiration, hope, courage, and strength.

— Edward A. Beiersdorf

All know that the drop merges into the ocean but few know that the ocean merges into the drop.

— Kabir

The stars go down to rise upon some other shore,
And bright in heaven's jeweled crown they shine forevermore.

— J. L. McCreery

The best advice I can offer... is... We learn as we go.
We do our best and hope it will turn out okay.

— Judy Blume

I suppose my general philosophy of life is trying not to be
negative, only to be positive, and not wasting time and effort
on things in the past that I cannot change, and looking
forward to the future over which I may have some influence.

— Angela Rippon

My philosophy of life is to treat people
in the way that I would like to be treated
and to give as much pleasure to others in
life as they have given to me.

— Lady Elizabeth Anson

Take time to dream —
it is hitching a wagon to a star.

— Old Irish Prayer

My philosophy is "Slow down, simplify, and be kind."

— Naomi Judd

My lesson in life has been learning to listen. Almost everyone has something of value to teach you. You can learn about life from the most unexpected sources, even children. It's a wise man who goes to others for help. Everyone was a beginner at some point in his life; even our teachers were once pupils.

— Chuck Norris

We were privileged to meet great teachers... who pushed our horizon wider, gave us greater openness of mind and a more flexible way of thinking. They challenged us to see the star and follow the gleam.

— Ethel Percy Andrus

My philosophy is this: Many things shine like stars. Memories, moments, high hopes, wonderful people, perfect words. If you let them, they'll inspire you, bring peace your way, and brighten your life.

— Douglas Pagels

Indeed, everybody wants to be a wow,
but not everybody knows exactly how.

— Ogden Nash

Never lose your capacity for enthusiasm ■ Never lose your capacity for indignation ■ Never judge people, don't type them too quickly; but in a pinch never first assume that a man is bad; first assume always that he is good and that at worst he is in the gray area between bad and good ■ Never be impressed by wealth alone or thrown by poverty ■ If you can't be generous when it's hard to be, you won't be when it's easy ■ The greatest builder of confidence is the ability to do something — almost anything — well ■ When that confidence comes, then strive for humility; you aren't as good as all that ■ And the way to become truly useful is to seek the best that other brains have to offer. Use them to supplement your own, and be prepared to give credit to them when they have helped ■ The greatest tragedies in world and personal events stem from misunderstandings ■ ANSWER: communicate ■

— Gordon Dean

I don't have enough words, but I also want to wish to all of you: Try to find happiness in every day. At least once, smile to each other every day. And say just one extra time that you love the person who lives with you. Just say, "I love you." It's so great. Okay?

— Ekaterina Gordeeva

Only from the heart can you touch the sky.

— Rumi

I need not hope for better times,
But better eyes to see with;
I need not wish for truer friends.
Or nicer folks to be with.

My life grows sweeter, day by day,
When I have learned to live it,
And happiness will come to me
When I have learned to give it.

— Henry P. Lorenz

Give of yourself, give as much as you can! And you can always give something, even if it is only kindness! If everyone were to do this and not be as mean with a kindly word, then there would be much more justice and love in the world. Give and you shall receive, much more than you would have ever thought possible.

— Anne Frank

I am not much concerned
With what days bring to me;
Far more important, I have learned, is
What I give them.

— Emma Wilson Emery

The measure of a life, after all, is not its duration but its donation.

— Corrie Ten Boom

Good deeds will shine as the stars of heaven.

— Chalmers

Unless a man has something to lift,
he can never find out how strong he is.

— Opie Read

I think a hero is an ordinary individual who finds the strength
to persevere and endure in spite of overwhelming obstacles.

— Christopher Reeve

I am bigger than anything that can happen to me. All these
things — sorrow, misfortune, and suffering, are outside my
door. I am in the house and I have the key.

— Charles F. Lummis

I can do anything. I can be anything. No one ever told me
I couldn't. No one ever expressed this idea that I was limited
to any one thing, and so I think in terms of what's possible,
not impossible.

— Whoopi Goldberg

Oh man! There is no planet, sun or star could hold you,
if you but knew what you are.

— Ralph Waldo Emerson

Like most people, there have always been two differing fellows under my vest. One personality serious minded, even shadowed with melancholy. The other fellow merryhearted, optimistic, even a bit reckless but able to fling worry to the winds. Years ago these two persons in my breast came to a compromise. Now they live at peace, the one exercising a wholesome restraint upon the other. When the serious fellow is inclined to worry the other says: "Cross no bridge till you come to it!" And the lighthearted fellow has been right, almost always. *He* has the better credit with me. I accept his counsel. I do not borrow trouble from the future. All the same, now and then I have to reckon with the serious fellow — he keeps me fairly prudent — but it is the merryhearted lad within who has taught me to grow younger with the years.

— Irving Bacheller

Twixt optimist and pessimist,
The difference is droll;
The optimist sees the doughnut,
The pessimist sees the hole.

— McLandburgh Wilson

Life is too good to waste a day.
It's up to you to make it sweet.

— Sadie Delany

Man is his own star.
— Beaumont and Fletcher

I'd planned to clean the house today ■ And store all the winter things away ■ But a little girl called out merrily ■ So my task must wait till she's tired of me ■

I'd thought I'd polish all the floors ■ And finish a hundred household chores ■ But a little boy wanted a story read ■ His dinner cooked and his puppies fed ■

With fields full of clover and the apple trees ■ The rosy richness of a springtime breeze ■ I forgot all the work that I'd planned to do ■ And just loafed in the meadow till the day was through ■

Why the tasks aren't finished I can't explain ■ I try to feel sorry but all is in vain ■ All the rapture I've known I just wouldn't miss ■ For no day will be as happy as this ■

— Edna B. Hawkins

When he grows up, I don't think he'll recall ■ How, on a sapphire morning in the fall ■ Dust tumbled up and down the stair ■ And smudges lined the woodwork here and there ■ While he and I ran hand in hand together ■ Carefree, into the bright October weather ■ I hope my son looks back upon today ■ And sees a mother who had time to play ■ Whether the work was done, or it was not ■ Who realized chores are sometimes best forgot ■ There will be years for cleaning house and cooking ■ But little boys grow up when we're not looking ■

— Barbara Overton Christie

Heaven is now, stars shine on earth.

— Thomas Campion

At the end of your life, you will never regret not having passed one more test, not winning one more verdict, or not closing one more deal. You will regret time not spent with a husband, a child, a friend, or a parent.

— Barbara Bush

Did you ever hear someone on his deathbed say: "I wish I'd spent more time at the office?"

— Anonymous

If, by gaining knowledge, we destroy our health, we labor for a thing that will be useless in our hands. He that sinks his vessel by overloading it, though it be with gold, and silver, and precious stones, will give his owner but an ill account of his voyage.

— John Locke

One way to live happily ever after is not to be after too much.

— Anonymous

It is the spirit of a person that hangs above him like a star in the sky.

— George Matthew Adams

We are putting too much weight on what we can buy for money, unmindful of the fact that the best things of this life are free.

— Opie Read

Enough is great riches.

— Danish Proverb

It isn't the cut of the clothes you wear ■ Nor the stuff out of which they are made ■ Though chosen with taste and fastidious care ■ And it isn't the price that you paid ■ It isn't the size of your pile in the bank ■ Nor the number of cars that you own... ■ But he who makes somebody happy, each day ■ And he who gives heed to distress ■ Will find satisfaction, the richest of pay ■ For it's service that measures success ■

— Anonymous

"You just can't have everything you want all the time — life isn't like that. Do you understand?"

"Oh yes, Papa. We understand," they said.

He talked to them about "counting their blessings," which meant enjoying the things they had instead of forever wanting more and more and more.

— The Berenstain Bears

Darkness makes us aware of the stars, and so when dark hours arise, they may hold a bright and lovely thing, we might never have known otherwise.

— Peter A. Lea

We cannot always have what we want, and we must prepare for and accept those changes over which we have no control.

— Arthur Ashe

I've figured my blessings but little, I fear;
My cares I have counted each day and each year.
Forgotten the pleasure, the pain I have kept,
Forever in mind ev'ry moment I wept.
The loss I remember, the sorrow recall,
The happiness I hardly remember at all.
But now I have taken a balance at last,
The joys and griefs of the present and past.
I've figured my blessings, I've set them apart
In a book I am keeping, the book of my heart.
I need not set down all the trouble and care,
I find I had already written it there.
But I had forgotten the love that is mine...
It took a whole column, the hate but a line.
The joy always greater, the grief always less,
I'm really astonished at the wealth I possess.

— From *Selah*

The sun is but a morning's star. To be awake is to be alive. If the day and night are such that you greet them with joy, and life is more starry... that is your success.

— Henry David Thoreau

Opportunists take now for an answer.

— Bob Talbert

If you have hard work to do,
    Do it now.
Today the skies are clear and blue,
Tomorrow clouds may come in view,
Yesterday is not for you;
    Do it now.
If you have kind words to say,
    Say them now.
Tomorrow may not come your way,
Do a kindness while you may,
Loved ones will not always stay;
    Say them now.
If you have a smile to show,
    Show it now.
Make hearts happy, roses grow,
Let the friends around you know
The love you have before they go;
    Show it now.

— Anonymous

Twenty years from now you will be more disappointed by the things
you didn't do than by the ones you did do. So throw off the bowlines.
Sail away from the safe harbor. Catch the trade winds in your sails.
Explore. Dream. Discover.

— Anonymous

Look upon the day-star moving, life and tyme are worth improving,
seize the moments while they stay, seize and use them, lest ye lose them.

— Motto on an Old Sundial

Most of us miss out on life's big prizes.
The Pulitzer. The Nobel. Oscars. Tonys.
Emmys. But we're all eligible for life's small
pleasures. A pat on the back. A kiss behind
the ear. A four-pound bass. A full moon.
An empty parking space. A crackling fire.
A great meal. A glorious sunset... Don't fret
about copping life's grand awards. Enjoy its
tiny delights. There are plenty for all of us.

— Anonymous

Life is an opportunity, benefit from it ■ Life is a beauty,
admire it ■ Life is bliss, taste it ■ Life is a dream, realize it ■
Life is a challenge, meet it ■ Life is a duty, complete it ■ Life
is a game, play it ■ Life is costly, care for it ■ Life is wealth,
keep it ■ Life is love, enjoy it ■ Life is mystery, know it ■
Life is a promise, fulfill it ■ Life is sorrow, overcome it ■
Life is a song, sing it ■ Life is a struggle, accept it ■ Life is
a tragedy, confront it ■ Life is an adventure, dare it ■ Life
is luck, make it ■ Life is too precious, do not destroy it ■
Life is life, fight for it! ■

— Mother Teresa

Though my soul may set in darkness, it will rise in perfect light;
I have loved the stars too fondly to be fearful of the night.

— An Old Astronomer to His Pupil

Do not damage the earth or the sea or the trees.

— Revelation 7:3 (NRSV)

Do your part for the planet. Do all the things you know you "should" do. Our grandchildren's children will either have words of praise for our efforts and our foresight, or words that condemn us for forgetting that they must live here long after we are gone. Don't overlook the obvious: This is not a dress rehearsal. This is the real thing. Our presence has an impact, but our precautions do, too. And the environment means the world to us.

— Douglas Pagels

UNLESS someone like you
cares a whole awful lot,
nothing is going to get better.
It's not.

— Dr. Seuss

There was, on one star, on one planet, on mine,
the Earth, a little prince to be consoled!

— Antoine de Saint-Exupéry

I expect to pass through this life but once. If, therefore, there be any kindness I can show, or any good thing I can do to any fellow being, let me do it now. Let me not defer or neglect it, for I shall not pass this way again.

— Stephen Grellet

If I should not walk this way again I'd like to have it said I did the little things beneath my hand. When I am dead I shall not know the things they say of me who went my way in this bright world and loved it so; but this I hope: that they will say I found that duty pleasant that was nearest me and that my hand on someone's shoulder made them go courageously.

— Frances Stockwell Lovell

My creed is this: Happiness is the only good. The place to be happy is here. The time to be happy is now. The way to be happy is to make others so.

— Robert G. Ingersoll

You only live once, but if you work it right, once is enough.

— Joe E. Lewis

Your name will be as legible on the hearts you leave behind, as the stars on the brow of the evening.

— Chalmers

If I Had My Life to Live Over

I'd like to make more mistakes next time. I'd relax, I would limber up. I would be sillier than I have been this trip. I would take fewer things seriously. I would take more chances. I would climb more mountains and swim more rivers. I would eat more ice cream and less beans. I would perhaps have more actual troubles, but I'd have fewer imaginary ones.

You see, I'm one of those people who lives sensibly and sanely hour after hour, day after day. Oh, I've had my moments, and if I had it to do over again, I'd have more of them. In fact, I'd try to have nothing else. Just moments, one after another, instead of living so many years ahead of each day. I've been one of those persons who never goes anywhere without a thermometer, a hot water bottle, a raincoat, and a parachute. If I had it to do over again, I would travel lighter than I have.

If I had my life to live over, I would start barefoot earlier in the spring and stay that way later in the fall. I would go to more dances. I would ride more merry-go-rounds. I would pick more daisies.

— Nadine Stair

If I had my life to live over, I'd make the same mistakes, only sooner.

— Tallulah Bankhead

Every night come out these envoys of beauty, and light the universe with their admonishing smile.

— Ralph Waldo Emerson

Even if you have a good excuse for giving up, remember that all the rewards go to those who stick till they get what they are after.

— *Boys' World*

It's not the things I
       failed to do
That make me wipe
       this eye —
It's things I should and
       could have done
And simply failed
       to try.

— Rebecca McCann

WOULDA-COULDA-SHOULDA

All the Woulda-Coulda-Shouldas
Layin' in the sun,
Talkin' 'bout the things
They woulda-coulda-shoulda done...
But those Woulda-Coulda-Shouldas
All ran away and hid
From one little *did*.

— Shel Silverstein

Climb high, climb far, your goal the sky, your aim the star.

— Anonymous

It is never too late to be what you might have been.

— George Eliot

All our lives are, in some sense, a "might have been." The very best of us must feel, I suppose, in sad and thoughtful moments, that he might have been transcendently nobler, and greater and loftier than he is. But while life lasts, every "might have been" should lead... to a "may be and will be yet!"

— Frederick William Farrar

It's never too late — in fiction or in life — to revise.

— Nancy Thayer

I know a smiling old lady, who says she has made it a life habit to expect, every morning when she awakes, to have a glorious day. She says she looks toward the coming day as she would toward a journey she was taking, and she is always expecting some new delight, some wonderful experience. She says that the very thought that the day holds beautiful things in store for those who expect them, for those who believe they are coming to them, has been a constant inspiration. It has helped to bring her the very things she expects.

— O. S. Marden

No star is ever lost we once have seen,
We always may be what we might have been.

— Adelaide A. Proctor

If you come to a thing with no preconceived notions of what that thing is, the whole world can be your canvas. Just dream it, and you can make it so. I believe I belong wherever I want to be, in whatever situation or context I place myself.

— Whoopi Goldberg

Be creative!
You're the artist here.
You're the one who can
brush away the clouds
and make the sun shine.
Paint your own picture,
choose your own colors.
And forget all that
business about having to
stay between the lines.

— Douglas Pagels

You have your brush, you have your colors,
you paint paradise, then *in* you go.

— Nikos Kazantzakis

And so in this exterior darkness, I was interiorly illumined!

— St. Thérèse of Lisieux

God grant me the serenity
To accept the things I cannot change;
The courage to change the things I can;
And the wisdom to know the difference.

— Reinhold Niebuhr

What matters is that you can move on, you can grow,
you can do better in the future.

— Kelsey Grammer

When I look to the future, I see more possibilities than limitations.

— Christopher Reeve

You are always nearer the divine and the true sources of your power
than you think.... Every place is under the stars, every place is the
center of the world.

— John Burroughs

We think, we feel, we are; and light, as of a star... is given;
We look not outward, but within, and think not quite to end as we begin.

— Edmund Clarence Stedman

The Creeds are writ: — Now you must say
Which is your creed for every day.

— Henry M. Rogers

Well, this is the end of a perfect day,
Near the end of a journey, too;
But it leaves a thought that is big and strong,
With a wish that is kind and true.

— Carrie Jacobs Bond

Often when you think you're at the end of something,
you're at the beginning of something else. I've felt that
many times. My hope for all of us is that "the miles we go
before we sleep" will be filled with all the feelings that
come from deep caring — delight, sadness, joy, wisdom —
and that in all the endings of our life, we will be able to
see the new beginnings.

— Fred Rogers

And as the evening twilight fades away,
The sky is filled with stars, invisible by day.
— Henry Wadsworth Longfellow

(Acknowledgments continued from page 4)

BLUE MOUNTAIN ARTS, INC., P.O. Box 4549, Boulder, Colorado 80306.